A YEAR OF MINIMALISM

A YEAR OF

MINIMALISM

Daily Practices to
Embrace Mindful Living

TIA PATTERSON

ROCKRIDGE
PRESS

For general information on our other products and services or to obtain technical support, please contact our Customer Care Department within the United States at (866) 744-2665, or outside the United States at (510) 253-0500.

Rockridge Press publishes its books in a variety of electronic and print formats. Some content that appears in print may not be available in electronic books, and vice versa.

Interior and Cover Designer: Erik Jacobsen
Art Producer: Hannah Dickerson
Editor: Brian Sweeting
Production Manager: Chris Gage

Author photo courtesy of Billie Board Photography

Paperback ISBN: 978-1-63807-373-4
eBook 978-1-63878-023-6
R0

**Dedication:
For you.**

CONTENTS

There is no place like home.

—*L. Frank Baum,* The Wonderful Wizard of Oz

INTRODUCTION

You are here. Greetings to you, and congratulations for saying *yes* to the call of your spirit to explore a lifestyle in mindful pursuit of minimalism.

Before we start on this journey, take a moment to pause and think about what a minimalist lifestyle would mean for you. Before I began my own journey, this is what minimalism originally meant for me:

MINIMALISM 101

1. Remove physical clutter by buying and owning less stuff.

2. Allow for more open space, time, and energy in life.

3. Add more value and meaning to these free and open areas, and thereby experience more personal joy.

4. *Optional:* Include #mariekondoapproved on all shared Instagram stories and photos showcasing new minimalist space.

CONNECT WITH YOUR INNER MINIMALIST

My learning experience with minimalism began two years ago, when I sensed that some type of significant change was upon me and my way of life. After moving with my family into a smaller home, I decided to embrace the art of minimalist living. I bought less and let go of things that no longer served me or brought me joy, from old furniture and unworn clothing to old Tupperware— you know, those few pieces without matching lids.

I looked around and noticed that my daily living space was more simple, free, and open to receive things that carried more meaning and purpose in my life. Still, I was lost on how to genuinely feel, to coexist in this space, to thrive personally. Overwhelming clutter still managed to find a place in my home. My true, forever home. *The home that is within me.*

Minimalism is the study of simple life.
Simple life = a mindful way of living.

Minimalism was the opening that invited me to become familiar with the path that would continually lead me back home to reconnect with my heart. I said to myself, "Okay, this practice goes beyond the physical, so what's next?" After much research and receiving of insight, I gathered thoughtful tools and techniques to aid me in the daily walk of *mindfully* living my journey back home. Now, with an intention of support and encouragement, I seek to share with you what I learned (and continue to learn).

Each calendar day in this book includes a simple practice, reflection, positive affirmation, or inspiring quote. All are tools to help you discover what a mindful way of living looks like, feels like, tastes like, and sounds like, with insight to embrace the realization that all of it starts with *you*. You know what resonates with you and what should be offered back in love, because you are the most authentic author of your life and can determine how it evolves with time.

The tools found here will be more effective if your mindful approach is grounded in intentionality and consistency, with respect for grace, patience, and compassion for self; I learned this fact through my personal experience and much consideration. It's also helpful to designate a journal specifically for your personal record during this one-year journey. You may experience improvement in your mental and emotional well-being. However, the daily offerings provided here are not a replacement for professional therapy or medical treatment, both of which can be extremely helpful for your holistic health.

FINDING YOU, AGAIN

So now I ask you: What do you seek to find along your yellow brick road back home?

- Is it a better connection with the implicit nature of your being, what defines you, and how you naturally *think* and exist in this world?
- Is it the ability to allow the desires of your *heart* to be your guide back to your most natural form of art and the simplest beauty of just being you?

- Is it the *courage* to live in alignment with the purpose of your soul and to cease the mindless chase of acquiring things that are not truly valuable to you?

WELCOME, DEAR SEEKER, TO YOUR MINDFUL YEAR OF MINIMALISM

I hope this book meets you as a resourceful companion, one full of inspiration and encouragement to take simple daily steps to live more presently and nurture gratitude and joy in a home that is inherently of you. *For there is no other place like it.*

JANUARY

Reconnect at the root of the simple and beautiful foundation of who you are by embracing yourself in unconditional love, attention, and care.

1

—

NEW YEAR INTENTION

I dedicate this year to returning to the home embedded in the heart of my true identity—for there is my true place in the world.

2

JANUARY

—

GROUND YOUR ENERGY

Close your eyes. Inhale and exhale deeply until you relax. Imagine roots growing out of your feet and going deep into the earth. Receive the energy of the earth as it flows up through your body. You are connected and supported by the universe. All is well.

3

JANUARY

SET THE MORNING MOOD

Create a morning routine or ritual for self-care. This can be a very simple practice that allows you to enjoy 5 to 10 minutes with yourself at the start of each day.

4

JANUARY

CLEANSE YOUR ENERGY

Take a shower. As the water flows, imagine it cleansing your mind and energetic body of the clutter of thoughts from the day.

5

—

BREATH = POWER

Your heart holds a flame of desire. Deepen your breathing with slow inhales and exhales. This connects you with the powerful force of air that blows to keep your inner flame ablaze. You have the power to connect and simply be.

6

JANUARY

—

AFFIRM YOUR TRUTH

Write down one positive affirmation of your choice. Repeat it for one minute in the morning, at noon, and at night, right before bed. When you create your affirmation, replace "I will" with "I am"—for example, "I will live my truth" becomes "I am my truth."

7

JANUARY

———

Within you, there is a stillness and a sanctuary to which you can retreat at any time and be yourself.

—*Hermann Hesse*

8

JANUARY

———

BE YOU

You are a *being*. You simply and physically exist in this human experience called life. *Being you* is your call to action. You are in control of that action. Write the story. Make the choices.

9
JANUARY

—

ATTITUDE OF GRATITUDE

What basic needs are met in your life, and what makes you grateful for each one? In your journal or using a notes app on your phone, write one to three sentences for each need, describing why you are grateful for it.

10
JANUARY

—

MIND YOUR GARDEN

Your garden is part of you, part of your home. Are you nurturing it? Do you water it with love and acceptance for how it grows? What type of fruit does it produce? Is that fruit rotting, or is it life-sustaining? Do you share your harvest with others?

11
JANUARY

—

A BATH DATE

Draw yourself a warm bath. Add Epsom or pink Himalayan salt. Light candles. Turn on music. Bring in flowers. Close your eyes. Feel the stillness of the water as it holds you.

12
JANUARY

—

SPEAK OUT

While driving, riding on the train or bus, walking, or biking, refrain from listening to any form of media. As your thoughts start to come to you in the silence, speak them out, even if it's just a whisper. It may seem awkward at first, but you may be surprised by how light the conversation (and you) become.

13
JANUARY

—

A LOVE NOTE

Recall a simple moment when you did something for yourself out of love. Maybe you took a second glance at yourself in the mirror, laughed at a funny thought, or put on warm socks when you felt cold. Now, tell yourself, "Thank you."

14
JANUARY

—

MINGLE WITH THE EARTH

Go outside. Breathe in the strength of the trees. Feel the warmth of the sun. Touch the flowers. Dig your fingers into the soil. Mother Earth seeks to hold you in a secure and loving embrace. Embody her free spirit of love.

15
JANUARY

—

SECURE THE FOUNDATION

Is there something in your home that needs mending so that it functions properly? Maybe you have an unsteady bookshelf, an open patch in a screen door, or a flickering lightbulb. When you set aside time to address those small (but irritating) concerns, it can help you feel more together and secure about your ability to meet the simple needs in life.

16
JANUARY

—

AFFIRM THIS THREE TIMES:

I am.
I am being.
Being, I am.
Being, am I.

17

—

A DREAM REALIZED

This month we celebrate Dr. Martin Luther King Jr., a man who had a dream. Record one of your dreams and read it back aloud to yourself in front of a mirror. Witness your dream as a reflection of your soul.

18

JANUARY

—

MINDFUL SNOOZE

Take a nap today. Find time—even if it's just a 20-minute timed session—to lie down and rest in a quiet place. Allow your conscious mind to surrender in peaceful slumber.

19

JANUARY

DANCE YOUR HEART OUT

Boogie barefoot to music for 10 to 15 minutes or move your hands to the beat as if you're directing its flow. Don't think—let loose and just feel. If you need dance inspiration, check out the Purple Heart Club on Instagram (@josiahbell).

20

JANUARY

YOUR WORD IS YOUR BOND

Connect with yourself, and *your self* will connect with the world. Make a bulleted list of how you connect with your life in this world: likes, dislikes, interests, hobbies, goals, strengths, past wins. Next, make a bulleted list of how you connect with other people, places, and things. Notice any differences, similarities, and patterns.

21

JANUARY

—

AFFIRM THIS THREE TIMES:

I am everything I need.
I am just me.
I am here.
I am.

22

JANUARY

—

DRINK TEA

Brew yourself a cup of tea. With each sip, feel the warmth of the tea as it flows through your body. Close your eyes and relax in the simple moment of flow.

23
JANUARY

LET GO OF EXPIRED GOODS

What was good for you at one time may not be anymore. Some ideas or beliefs you hold about your identity can expire in their freshness, much like the food in your kitchen. Search your fridge and pantry for any out-of-date produce, canned food items, or unused goods. Then, throw them away—along with those expired thoughts that are no longer healthy to digest!

24
JANUARY

—

CONNECT WITH YOUR HIGHEST SELF

Your highest self is your truest, most authentic self, above any worldly attachment. Journal about what you believe your highest self looks like and feels like. Show compassion and love for all parts of you for your highest good.

25
JANUARY

—

LIVE ATTRACTIVELY

Focus less on what you're attracting in life. Realize how naturally attractive you are. You are the story of your own life. You are the unique vibration of musical notes to your life song.

26
JANUARY

EMBRACE YOUR INNER CHILD

You start to collect mind baggage as a child. Think of how heavy that must have been, and consider why you may still struggle to carry it now. Recall a specific time in your childhood when you were afraid, sad, in pain, or lost. Give your younger self a loving hug. Say to yourself, "I see you. You are protected."

27
JANUARY

ENERGY FLOW

Stretch your body. Feel free to try some simple yoga poses, such as child's pose, forward bend, mountain pose, squat, downward dog, or warrior. Another option is to position yourself in a seated position or lie on your back, forming an X with your arms and legs. Concentrate on the relaxed sensation of your muscles as your energy flows freely through the open channels in your body. This helps create a more supportive flow of energy from your mind into your body.

28
JANUARY

—

YOU ARE A WORK OF ART

Draw a picture of yourself. It can be a portrait, an abstract thought, an arrangement of colors, a shape made of words, or something else. Illustrate whatever you feel is the best representation of you.

29
JANUARY

—

BREAK HABIT

Change up the order of how you do one simple task during the day. Switch up your makeup, shaving, or face-washing routine. Groom your hair before getting dressed. Drink a glass of water before eating breakfast (or vice versa). Take a different route to work or school. Help keep your mind fresh and alert to break free from habitual thinking.

30
JANUARY

—

DEATH AND GROWTH

There is death in growth, and there is growth in death. Make a list of thoughts that make you feel limited, angry, anxious, worthless, or defeated. Burn the list or rip it into tiny paper shreds. Reflect on how the thoughts have undergone a conscious death in your mind. They may rise again as memories, but ultimately, they are dead—unable to grow any more as true affirmations of your heart.

31
JANUARY

—

Wisdom begins at the end.

—Daniel Webster

FEBRUARY

Recall your worthiness to live a life of abundance simply by being you. Minimalism at its finest.

1

—

BECOME THE FIRST NARRATOR OF YOUR DAY

How do you spend the first moments of your morning? What do you think about yourself? How will you go about your tasks for the day? Take back your power by controlling the things you can and releasing the things you can't.

2

FEBRUARY

—

RECOGNIZE A SENSE OF BEAUTY IN EVERY DETAIL

Take some time to get outside if you can. Notice the trees, the flowers, the color of the sky, the playful squirrels, the flight of the birds. Sense that you are a natural beauty, existing right along with all you see.

3

FEBRUARY

MOVE YOUR BODY

If you're able to, go for a run or a swim. Do a TikTok dance or simply roll your ankles and wrists. When you move your physical body, you move and activate your energy. You create a natural flow of sensations in your body that makes you feel good, inviting more creative thought and expression.

4

FEBRUARY

RELEASE

When your tummy is upset, you have a natural urge to release. Your mind can also become upset by what you're feeding it and require a release. Write down on toilet paper the thought or belief that's creating a funk in your mind. Toss it into the toilet and declare it released from your energy as you flush it away. Release that #hit!

5
FEBRUARY

DOODLE YOUR THOUGHTS

Gather drawing utensils and paper. Close your eyes and take three deep breaths. Draw whatever enters your mind first. Don't be technical. The basic art of yourself is enough.

6
FEBRUARY

WATCH THE SUNSET

As you watch the sun go down, put to rest any troubling concerns of your day. Simply enjoy the beauty and calmness of the day coming to an end.

7

FEBRUARY

—

AFFIRM THIS THREE TIMES:

I am space for myself.
I am beauty inside out.
I am the reality I desire.

8

FEBRUARY

—

GREET YOURSELF

When you find yourself doing a task that requires little thought, say to yourself, "Hello!" You can say it aloud or simply think it. Ask yourself how you're doing and what's been on your mind. Wait and listen for a response from within. Converse openly with yourself without any judgment. You may be surprised by what you learn about yourself while you're simply doing the dishes.

9

FEBRUARY

—

SET HEALTHY BOUNDARIES

Boundaries help create a safe space in which to live authentically. You can create boundaries for who and what has access to your thoughts and energy. A healthy boundary can even exist between your heart and your mind.

10

FEBRUARY

—

SILENT BATH

Take a bath and sit silently in stillness. Allow your mind to be as still as the water.

11
FEBRUARY

—

CLEAN UP

Perform a cleaning task in your home. As you clean, visualize the dust, clutter, and debris being removed from your energy.

12
FEBRUARY

—

MEMORIES ARE GIFTS OF THE MIND

Recall your earliest memories. For each year between the ages of 4 and 10, journal about one particular memory that you have. Review your list. Is there a pattern? Are they memories of simple moments or grand moments? Is love present?

13

—

THE NATURAL BEAUTY OF LIFE

Add more life to your home with fresh flowers from your garden or plants from a nearby market. Inviting nature into your space helps you breathe more easily and appreciate the simple beauty that is of the world (and within you).

14
FEBRUARY

—

BECOME FAMILIAR WITH YOURSELF

Love exists in familiarity, like the child who recognizes their parent at school pickup, or the dog that jumps with excitement when its owner returns home. When you become familiar with your true self, you connect in love, and acceptance and joy naturally follow.

15
FEBRUARY

—

If you don't like something, change it.
If you can't change it, change
your attitude.

—Maya Angelou

16
FEBRUARY

—

CHOOSE SAFETY OVER FEAR

Choose to acknowledge the simple, positive aspects of your present life with gratitude. This might include being thankful for the food in your kitchen, the bed that you sleep on, or the money in your bank account. Embodying the energy of gratitude for your present abundance attracts even more good things for you in the future.

17
FEBRUARY

—

RELEASE DISTRACTIONS WITH
ALTERNATE NOSTRIL BREATHING

Close your right nostril, and inhale through your left nostril.
At the top of your inhale, switch and close your left nostril,
exhaling out of your right nostril. Inhale through your right
nostril, and then close it and exhale out of your left nostril.
Inhale through your left nostril, then close it and exhale
out of your right nostril. Continue this practice for three to
five minutes.

18
FEBRUARY

—

BRING IT ON

Identify a present challenge or obstacle in your life. Visualize yourself react-
ing to it with a sense of calm, stability, and courage. Practice embodying that
balanced version of you as you continue throughout the day.

19
FEBRUARY

—

WELL-BEING

What makes you happy? Maybe it's eating a comforting meal, spending time
with friends, watching a movie about love, or reading an interesting book.
Create a log of things you do that bring you happiness. Feel free to revisit
your well of happiness when you're in search of a better mood.

20

THE GIFT OF LIFE

The present moment is a gift. You have more real and active control over your feelings and experiences in the here and now. The past can't be changed, and the future is only planned. What will you choose to do with your gift? Will you accept it with gratitude?

21

FEBRUARY

AFFIRM THIS THREE TIMES:

I am a container for divine abundance.
I am in alignment with my soul purpose.
I am dancing to the rhythm of my heart.

22

—

HYGIENE OF THE MIND

When you brush your teeth today, think about something in your life that acts like bacteria—a limitation that causes erosion in your life and blocks you from living out the brightest potential of who you are. Mindfully brush away those bacteria. Rinse and spit. Brighten your mind's smile.

23
FEBRUARY

—

A CROWDED ROOM = A CROWDED MIND

Declutter your bedroom. Remove dirty laundry. Organize your nightstand. Minimize the number of bed pillows. Because your bedroom is typically the place where you start and end each day, it can affect your mood and energy if it's overcrowded with too many things.

24
FEBRUARY

—

ADJUST YOUR PERSPECTIVE

Your shadow is one thing that you can't let go of—but you do have control over how you embrace it. Do you remember when you first became aware of yours? How did you feel? Were you nervous, scared, shy, confused, curious? Take time today to notice your shadow. How do you feel when you look at it now?

25
FEBRUARY

—

REMEMBER YOUR MAGIC

What are you searching for? Sit still and remember your gifts. Everything you need exists in you already. Just remember and believe.

26

FEBRUARY

Rather than being your
thoughts and emotions, be the
awareness behind them.

—Eckhart Tolle

27

FEBRUARY

LEGGO MY EGO

Your common sense (ego) seeks to help you survive and it evolves from experiences you have lived—but that doesn't mean that it's a genuine truth of your soul. Your soul and ego are naturally involved in your being. Do you choose to merely survive, or do you choose to thrive in your way of living?

28
FEBRUARY

—

OPEN YOUR MIND TO SEE

Close your eyes. Take a few deep breaths. Envision a door. This door leads to your most genuine and unique way of being. Walk closer, then open the door. Look down at your feet. With your first step, walk through that door. Take note of what you see, hear, and feel. Embrace this world of you for as long as you like. Journal your thoughts.

MARCH

Your existence is already enough.
Your passions help define the more to your
enough. This is your creativity.
Remember to connect with what lights you up.

1

MARCH

—

THE BOOK OF LIFE

Life is not perfect. Instead of trying to make everything in your life *just right*, release the need for perfection and *just write*. After all, you are the best author of your life.

2

MARCH

—

BREATHE IN CONFIDENCE, BREATHE OUT CONFUSION

Close your eyes. Take a deep breath in through your mouth, opening up your chest. Breathe out audibly, letting go of all tension and anxiety. Do this whenever your mind is getting too loud.

3

MARCH

SEE YOURSELF

Choose to be proud of yourself today—proud of how you exist in the world, and proud of how you choose to be you.

4

MARCH

CREATE SPACE FOR YOURSELF

Do you ever find yourself constantly giving to or creating for others, leaving little to offer yourself? Place your hands on your heart. Set an intention to hold space for your journey and your growth. Ask yourself, "How can I nurture myself to a healthier state?"

5

MARCH

———

ATTEND OR TUNE IN TO A SOUND BATH

Certain sounds contain healing frequencies for your mind and body. Meditate today and listen to binaural beats. With this type of music, a different sound frequency is sent to each ear, creating a mental state conducive to deep, relaxing meditation. You can find various hertz selections on YouTube, Spotify, and Apple Music.

6

MARCH

———

WATER AND GROW

Drink more water today. As you prepare to drink each glass, set an intention for joy and fulfillment in your growth.

MARCH

AFFIRM THIS THREE TIMES:

I am my home source of inspiration.
I am confident that what I offer is enough.
I am my highest potential personified.

8

MARCH

REPLACE PRESSURE WITH PLEASURE

What is one thing you can tidy around your home that would serve as an incentive to enjoy a moment of pleasure? Some ideas: Clean your bathroom so you can enjoy a warm bath, dust a specific room (or even your entire home) so you can breathe better, or wash your bed linens for a night of cozy slumber.

9
MARCH

—

LIVE A LIFE OF EASE

Daydream by staring out of a window for at least five uninterrupted minutes.
You may be surprised by what you discover about yourself, effortlessly.

10
MARCH

—

BECOME MINDFUL OF YOUR EMOTIONAL TRIGGERS

Think of a recent unpleasant circumstance in your life. How did you respond?
What did your body naturally do in response? Take a moment to breathe
deeply and become aware of and present with that emotion. This will help
you adopt the practice of breathing deeply and staying present in a current
or future moment of conflict.

11
MARCH

—

NATURALLY SWEET

Your fruit in life is ripened by the intensity of belief in your thoughts. Cut up some orange or fruit slices and place them in your bath. Visualize the fruit as your personal desires. The bathwater is an extension of the water living inside you. Relax as the water is naturally sweetened by your flowing fruit.

12
MARCH

—

STEP OUT OF YOUR COMFORT ZONE

What does your comfort zone look like? How does it feel? Take a moment to envision an exit door. Place one part of your body (however small) outside this door. Reflect on any mental or physical sensations you feel.

13
MARCH

—

SHOW YOURSELF

Show up for yourself before you share yourself with the world. This morning, take some time to visualize and feel what brings you joy, makes you feel lighter, and nourishes you in love. Sit with the feelings as they flow through your body.

14
MARCH

—

TOUCH AND AGREE

After your bath or shower, gently massage your entire body with lotion or oil. Think about how your body is uniquely yours. With your touch, send love to your body and give thanks for its strength and beauty.

15
MARCH

—

The vibration of being who
you are and doing what you
love is magnetic. You will align
everything you need in your life
with that energy.

—*Maryam Hasnaa*

16

MARCH

—

BLANK CANVAS

If you had the opportunity for a do-over for any big decision in your life, what would you change? Your dreams are your opportunity to paint your life. Living your dreams is the masterpiece.

17

MARCH

—

WEAR YOUR BEAUTY FREELY

Wearing green today? Feel free to do your own thing. Wear something that makes you feel beautiful. Maybe it's lipstick, your favorite cap, or a positive attitude. Freely embrace how you wear beauty, despite what the world may expect or accept.

18
MARCH

—

THE MAGIC OF BELIEF

Think of a current challenge in your life. Release all the reasons why it won't work out, and believe the one reason it will. What you focus on grows. Eventually, evidence of your belief will show up in your life.

19
MARCH

—

TAKE A SEAT AT YOUR TABLE

In your journal, or using the notes app on your phone, create a table with two columns. In the first column, list all the needs in your life that are still outstanding. In the second column, list all the wants in your life that have been fulfilled. When you're done, take a seat at this table and explore the lists to discover what they may be telling you.

20
MARCH

—

IMAGINE YOU ARE A CAKE

What ingredients make up your basic layer? Consider what your frosting is
made of. How sweet is your existence? Should you add another cup of sugar?
No need to call a neighbor; you have everything you need, right in your
own pantry.

21
MARCH

—

AFFIRM THIS THREE TIMES:

I am a walking boundary, releasing
all that is not for me.
I am the change that seeks what is best for me.
I am the passion that lives within my heart.

22
MARCH

YOUR HEART ON A SLEEVE

Browse through your wardrobe as if you're shopping what's there for the first time. Make a mental note of any negative, uncomfortable, or shameful feelings that may arise when you come across certain clothing pieces. Gather up the emotional pile of garb and choose to donate it or throw it away.

23
MARCH

DIG AT THE ROOT

Explore the root of one of your possible escape habits (something you think about or do to avoid difficult or uncomfortable moments of being). These habits can hinder your creativity and your ability to fully and freely accept yourself. Ask yourself, "When did this behavior start? What does it offer me? What does it try to hide about me?"

24
MARCH

—

SLOW DOWN, AGAIN

Take a moment to clear your mind of activity. Simply close your eyes for 10 minutes. Rest and retreat to an empty space of dark solitude where you are the light.

25
MARCH

—

THE MARRIAGE OF THE MIND

Say "I do" to your own self. Declare yourself as a lifelong recipient of your unconditional love, trust, and commitment. Treat today as your honeymoon.

26
MARCH

LIVING NATURALLY IS SIMPLE

Watch an animal or a small insect at work or play until it departs.

27
MARCH

RENOVATION OF THE MIND

Break down the walls of limitation that you have erected in your mind. Create more open space for the desires of your heart to expand there and influence your thoughts. Free your mind, elevate your heart, and live in the new foundation of your wisdom.

28
MARCH

—

The simplest things are often the truest.

—*Richard Bach*

29
MARCH

—

TRY SOMETHING NEW

Do something that you wouldn't usually do or something you've never tried. Try a new food. Listen to a different type of music or podcast. Watch a different movie genre. Open yourself up to the possibility of accepting something new about yourself.

30
MARCH

—

TRUST YOUR YES

Have you ever shared an idea that fiercely lit you up, only to have it shut down or harshly ridiculed by someone else? Choose to protect your energy. Allow yourself to feel the emotion in your body. Your full-body *yes* is often the only validation you should seek (and need).

31
MARCH

—

LOVE IS SIMPLE

Tell yourself, "I love you."

APRIL

Trust in the power of your creativity.
You have what it takes to set the scene
for the play that is your life.
Be inspired as its director and leading actor.

1

APRIL

PLAY LIKE A CHILD

While meditating, envision your younger self. You're free to create and experience the world's simple joys. Practice letting go of boundaries and limits on creativity within your mind. Follow your inner child while dancing in the rain, jumping in a puddle, or splashing in the bath.

2

APRIL

TREAT YOURSELF GINGERLY

Drink a cup of ginger tea and set the intention to treat yourself with great care and patience throughout your journey today. Ginger tea helps increase your overall energy and removes toxic waste from your body.

3
APRIL

NOT ALL CONFLICT IS BAD

A bad day doesn't equate to a bad life. Forgive yourself. Free up space for love to reach your heart. All is well.

4
APRIL

CREATE A DIFFERENT NARRATIVE

Think about two or three moments in your life when you cried. Go back to those places in your mind, and laugh. Embrace hope in your tomorrow.

5

APRIL

YOU'RE DOING GREAT

Write down one accomplishment from yesterday that you're proud of.

6

APRIL

RETURN TO YOUR CREATIVITY

Lie down on your back. Close your eyes, and relax your body. Breathe normally. If you're able, place your hands on your lower abdomen; feel the rhythm of your breath. With each flow of breath, imagine yourself riding a wave back to the shore of your creativity.

APRIL

The world as we have created it is a
process of our thinking. It cannot be
changed without changing our thinking.

—*Albert Einstein*

APRIL

CALL OUT YOUR FEAR

Have you ever felt intrigued by something, but lacked the courage to pursue
it? Name the fear that holds you back, and then release it in your mind. Call
back to yourself the power of belief in action.

9
APRIL

THE KEY TO IT ALL

Consider a circumstance in which you tend to seek confirmation or approval from an outside source. Take a breath and say to yourself:

"I am the key. I am the key to my kingdom. I am the key to open the doors of possibility. I am the key to set myself free!"

10
APRIL

YOGA TO RELEASE

Do a sensual yoga session on YouTube or make up your own feel-good routine. For example, gently trace your body with your fingers, or slowly massage your scalp.

11
APRIL

—

GAS YOURSELF UP

Choosing to simply be you in this life adds fuel to sustain your fire. This is your holy oil. Anoint yourself with the energy that simply comes from the source of who you are.

12
APRIL

—

BREATHE AND BE

With your inhale, take in any self-limiting thoughts you may have. Then, release those thoughts with your exhale. Create the freedom for yourself in your breath of fresh air.

13
APRIL

YOU CAN EAT YOUR CAKE, TOO

Eat something sweet. Sit in the moment, thinking of how you can experience joy and pleasure from the simple indulgence of being you. (You can even lick your fingers.) Don't be shy, you sweet thang, you!

14
APRIL

YOUR SPACE, YOUR TASTE

Who says your couch must sit in front of your TV, or that your bed has to be set up against a wall? Free yourself from conventional limitations, even when it comes to room design. Embrace your individuality, and rearrange your space in a way that makes tasteful sense to you.

15
APRIL

AFFIRM THIS THREE TIMES:

*I am the trust that I need
when I become lost.
I am the creator of my thoughts
and actions.
I am energy flowing in the
creativity of love.*

16
APRIL

—

LOVE IS NATURALLY CREATIVE

Spend some intimate time with a loved one, or take yourself on a date. Dance, write, paint, hike, run, have sex, or enjoy self-pleasure. Allow yourself freedom to let go and love what you do.

17
APRIL

—

WATER YOUR INTENT

Within the first hour of waking today, drink one full glass of water. Set an intention for how you choose to live today in gratitude.

18
APRIL

LIVE LIFE ON YOUR TERMS

If you have a moment of self-doubt, replace it with a truth. You can't mess up anything that's meant for you. Any decision you make has a purpose along your journey to the result.

19
APRIL

INVITE IN THE NATURAL LIGHT

Tidy the main living space in your home. At night, turn off all the artificial lights, then light a few candles in the space. The candlelight helps to create a mood of sensual calm that can help you wind down after a long day. Connect with the natural energy of light, and just relax in the moment.

20
APRIL

WE ARE ALL CONNECTED

Send someone you love a text of gratitude. This can be as simple as, "Thank you for being you."

21
APRIL

Knowing yourself is to be rooted in Being, instead of lost in your mind.

—*Eckhart Tolle*

22
APRIL

EARTH IS OUR SHARED, COLLECTIVE HOME

Spend time outside totally unplugged—no phone, no music, nothing but you and the wonderful sights and sounds of nature.

23
APRIL

EMBRACE YOUR UNIQUE BODY

Look in the mirror. Notice one thing you like or love about yourself. Feel free to give yourself a compliment. Flatter yourself to your heart's content.

24
APRIL

DELETE AND KEEP IT MOVING

Think of one person or account you follow on social media that, truthfully, bothers you. Delete it. Set a boundary, and claim back your discretion of interest.

25
APRIL

FORMATION IN PROGRESS

You are developing a fresh new perspective in life. You have the power to create your thoughts and rearrange your actions into a more fulfilling alignment. You pass Go many times in the game of life—don't be afraid to begin again.

26
APRIL

—

STILL TO FEEL

When your mind is still, you're more receptive to energy flowing naturally through you and to you. Still the noise so the simple vibration of what is yours finds you again.

27
APRIL

—

AFFIRM THIS THREE TIMES:

I am the gatekeeper of my power.
I am attractive to the blessings that seek me.
I am the fulfillment of my wildest dreams.

28
APRIL

DON'T BE AFRAID TO *ASK*

Take a moment to ask yourself a question today—any question at all. Be aware of what you may feel in your body or hear in your mind. Write your answer in your journal.

29
APRIL

MIND ON A BUDGET

Make emotional budget cuts. Simply declare that you can't afford stress, doubt, confusion, or negative energy. This will free up more room in your account to receive love. You can then choose to share your wealth in gratitude.

30
APRIL

—

WRITE IT OFF

Get in touch with your emotions, and journal about any shame that you carry. What painful experiences have you carried and kept hidden? What challenging feelings show up continually? Once your pain is out in the open, even just as words on paper, a lot of its power goes away.

MAY

*You have the power of free will to claim
the gift of who you are.*

1

MAY

SPEAK YOUR MIND

Have a conversation with yourself, and speak out loud. Your mind is worthy of having a voice in this world.

2

MAY

THE ESSENCE OF EFFORT

We often feel more productive when we *do* more. However, it's easy to become so busy with demands that we're rigid and resistant to change. What if *being productive* actually meant honoring your energy, a natural effort in which you're open and willing to flow into yourself and connect with your creative ideas and soul-inspired thoughts?

3
MAY

BREAK A SWEAT

Go for a light jog. Squat to an entire song. Do a forearm plank for one minute. Try to wall-sit for two minutes. Stretch both arms out in front of you and hold for five minutes if you can. It's perfectly fine to sweat the "small stuff" in your mind. Your endorphins will naturally release the pain and bring more pleasure.

4
MAY

DOES IT BELONG TO YOU?

We all have an energy of desire. Be mindful of the source of this energy. Are your wants in life original, or have they been copied and pasted? Are you trusting that what's yours will come or are you lusting after what someone else has already done?

5

STRETCH YOURSELF

Stretch to get to know yourself better. Allow yourself to freely move into different stretch positions that feel good and satisfying. Hold each position for as short or as long as you desire. Be conscious of your breath and let your motions flow.

6

IF YOU CAN DREAM IT, IT'S ALREADY YOURS

Call your dreams to you. Choose to believe in yourself, and set an intention to take small steps (no matter how small) in trust and gratitude.

MAY

AFFIRM THIS THREE TIMES:

I am powerful.
I am authentic.
I am special.
I am whole on my own.

MAY

MOTHER YOURSELF

Write a letter to your younger self. Tell yourself why you've always been worthy of living life your way. Nurture your self-esteem and confidence.

9

MAY

—

NOW DOESN'T NEED TOMORROW

Answer the call to release yourself from a fixation on future timelines (and past ones) with faith and surrender. You can feel happy and fulfilled right now—because now is when you have the most control over how you experience life.

10

MAY

—

LOVE IS FREE

What is one of your favorite self-care practices? Do it today—not because you deserve it or for any specific reason, but because it's always yours to receive. Loving yourself is a gift, not a goal.

11
MAY

—

SOCIAL MEDIA BREAK

Spend less time scrolling on social media. Overconsuming can lead to negative comparisons and feelings of guilt and frustration. Set a specific time during the day, such as during your lunch hour, for healthy social media access. Until then, close the apps.

12
MAY

—

YOU ARE THE MUSE

In your journal, describe one of the best compliments you've ever received, and consider why it makes you happy to this day. Have you received this compliment more than once? Do you believe it? Is it a validation of who you are, or is it a reflection of who you are?

13
MAY

—

SET THE STAGE

You are free to create whatever life you choose. Declare that you are not bound to external ideas of normalcy or acceptance. And don't be afraid to make a mess—consider this an opportunity to remember your magic.

14
MAY

—

FEELING SO FRESH AND SO CLEAN

There are lots of little things you can do around your home to increase your confidence. Make your bed in the morning to start the day with an accomplishment. Clean the mirrors in your home so you can see yourself better. Fold and put away your clothing so you have more wearable options. Think of the actions that will inspire you to say, "Hey, I clean up pretty nice!"

15
MAY

—

This is a wonderful day. I've
never seen this one before.

—*Maya Angelou*

16
MAY

—

RELAX YOUR ATTITUDE IN GRATITUDE

Where are your thoughts leading you today? What are you focused on? Remind yourself, "There are moments when I need to slow down and ground my energy." Rampant random thoughts indicate a lack of gratitude. Gratitude involves centering yourself back to your home frequency. This invites calmness and guidance.

17
MAY

—

SCRATCH THE AGENDA

Embrace the freedom to play and create for your personal joy and pleasure. Set aside any intention to produce a specific outcome. No outside approval or acceptance is required.

18
MAY

—

SHINING MOMENTS

Make note of moments during your life when you confidently expressed yourself, no matter what anyone else thought. You're here to shine in your purpose without apology or explanation.

19
MAY

—

EAT THOUGHTFULLY

Before preparing a snack or meal, ask yourself, "Is this in response to hunger or a craving?" Listen to your body when it signals fullness to you. Your body is a wise communicator of how much you require to be satisfied.

20
MAY

—

MIND IN ACTION

If you seek to be in control of your life, connect with your mind. Your thoughts are powerful. Still the mind and learn how to control intruding random thoughts. Then, take the director's chair of your movie.

21
MAY

—

AFFIRM THIS THREE TIMES:

I am taking back my life one thought at a time.
I am attractive to all that is for me.
I am strong enough to say no.

22
MAY

SEE YOURSELF

Using your phone or camera, record yourself cleaning a room, or simply take a set of before-and-after pictures to see your progress. When you become aware that you have the ability to get things done and to make something better than it was before, you gain more confidence in yourself.

23
MAY

SIT DOWN

We're often expected to *seek and find* what we are supposed to do or be in this world. Take a seat with yourself—and *let your purpose come* to you.

24
MAY

—

MULTITASKING IS OVERRATED

You may switch between multiple tasks quickly, hoping to get things done faster. This is an illusion. If you seek productivity, focus on one task at a time. More focus brings less stress and anxiety. This creates a calm space that willingly invites productive energy.

25
MAY

—

FULFILLMENT IS A FEELING

What lights you up? What stirs you? You may have many *things* in life, yet still lack inspiration or enthusiasm. You can be grateful and still yearn for more feelings of fulfillment. This is how you learn to embrace who you are.

26
MAY

—

TOOT YOUR OWN HORN

In your journal, describe yourself as if you were introducing yourself to a total stranger. List all the attributes that make you who you are.

27
MAY

—

Trust yourself. You know more
than you think you do.

—*Benjamin Spock*

28
MAY

———

PURPOSE IS ROOTED IN WONDER

Make a list of things you enjoyed doing as a child. Recalling the interests and hobbies you had when you were young—before anyone imposed ideals and suggestions—can connect you with what you truly love and enjoy.

29
MAY

———

TAKE BACK WHAT YOU OWN

Claim back your power and energy. Give back in love what does not belong to you. Act, think, and believe from the center of your home, your heart—and do so for the pleasure, fulfillment, and joy of your soul, not for the approval, attention, or acceptance of others. This is your life.

30
MAY

ASK

Find a quiet space. Relax, take a deep breath, and ask your-self, "What is my soul telling me I need right now?" Write it down in your journal.

31
MAY

—

YOU ARE THE COACH

Give yourself a pep talk. Repeat these words: "I step back into my home frequency. My authenticity. My divine self. I learn what I can control in life and how to flow with what I learn. This reminds me to tap into my full abilities, spiritually and energetically, so that I can live and share my truest self."

JUNE

*Embrace the power within to release what blocks
you and to align with your truest self.*

JUNE

TO CALM YOUR THOUGHTS, YOU MUST BECOME THEM

Thoughts are constantly flowing in your mind, and it can be difficult to calm them. You may try to still the mind, but the waves crash over you and take you under. If you learn the rhythm of the wave, you can direct its flow. You won't always get it right, but if you're willing to practice, you can learn to ride more gracefully, more often.

JUNE

WALK IT OUT

If you're able, get outside for a bit this morning. Inhale the fresh air. Move deliberately, and stay aware of the natural flow of your breath. If thoughts interfere, return to your breath. Continue to move forward calmly, and establish the tone for your day.

3
JUNE

___

WHERE THERE'S A WILL, THERE'S A WAY

When you set your mind to achieving something, you'll find a way to make it happen. You can practice and strengthen this mindset within the comfort of your home. You can wash and fold all of your dirty laundry. You can remove all the pet hair from your furniture. You can keep your house tidy with an active toddler. Nothing is impossible.

4
JUNE

___

TAKE IT EASY

Think of one simple thing you would like to accomplish today. By setting clear and reasonable intentions, you can exercise your willpower more easily.

5

JUNE

MEDITATION FOR RETURNING TO YOUR POWER

Close your eyes. Take a deep breath.

Imagine yourself inside a shell. You're hiding away from the busyness and stress of life.

Your courageous self comes to your aid like a gentle friend.

You hold your hand in the dark as you work together to emerge from the shell.

As you step into the light, you see yourself again and remember your power and worth.

Open your eyes. Drink water.

6

JUNE

—

RELEASE TO RECEIVE

When life seems to get hard or stressful, it's often because you're trying to hold on to a thought or feeling that is no longer in your best interest. A release must occur, creating more open space in your heart and mind so you can accept what's better for you with ease. Now, when you find yourself in a tough spot, ask, "What do I need to release?"

7

JUNE

—

Trust that your soul has a plan, and even if you can't see it completely, know that everything will unfold as it is meant to.

—*Deepak Chopra*

8
JUNE
—
LOOK WITHIN

Sometimes you may become discouraged on your path when you look around and compare your journey with someone else's. Stay faithful and committed to your unique path. Examine with your heart and soul. True fulfillment is found by looking within.

9
JUNE
—
EXPRESS YOURSELF

Exercise. Dance to a fast beat. Sing out at the top of your lungs. Paint a picture. Write a poem. Talk with someone you trust. Cry. Hum. All are healthy ways to allow the pent-up emotions of anger, stress, or anxiety to pass through and find release from your mind and body.

10
JUNE

—

KEEP THE PEACE

Let your thoughts come. Don't fight them away—instead, let them flow. Embrace this opportunity to learn your voice, which will allow you to recognize it and distinguish it from the noise that is not aligned with your soul. Build on your power to protect the peace in your home.

11
JUNE

—

YOUR BODY TALKS

Your body can help confirm your truth. When you experience an emotion, take note of your body's cues. Do you move or position yourself in response? Do you feel pain? Now, make a mental note. Maybe next time you'll notice a pattern of communication.

12
JUNE

—

SWITCH IT UP

When you're overwhelmed with doubt or fear, stop. Physically remove your-self from your current space. Give yourself a quick change of scenery, if only for a minute. Move outside or go into another room. Calm down, and focus on your past wins. Gain strength from that moment.

13
JUNE

—

YOU ARE NOT A DOORMAT

You are free to listen to ideas from others, but you don't have to accept them.

14
JUNE

—

MIND DETOX

Write down habits, ideas, and limitations that are no longer in your best interest. Close your eyes and say each unhealthy behavior out loud. Each time you voice one of your unhealthy behaviors, revisit why this is no longer good for you. Give thanks for the learning experience. Release it from your mind in gratitude.

15

JUNE

—

AFFIRM THIS THREE TIMES:

*I am responsible for my life.
I am ready to face challenges.
I am motivated to pursue
my passions in life.
I am in my personal power.*

16
JUNE

OH, HAPPY DAY

List five songs that make you feel happy. Listen to one of these songs now.

17
JUNE

YOUR HOME IS AN EXTENSION OF YOUR ENERGY

The energy held within you affects the environment of your home. When you have moments of personal release, it's a good idea to include your external home in that practice. You can do so by burning sage or palo santo sticks; these help clear the air and neutralize positive ions. Smudge the incense to clear the home of stagnant or unfulfilled energy, and set an intention to welcome in creativity, protection, and unconditional love.

18
JUNE

NOT TODAY

If a thought or action rubs you the wrong way, you can choose to withdraw your attention from it. Protect your energy. You can decide not to address an emotion or situation immediately every time it arises.

19
JUNE

R-E-S-P-E-C-T

What does self-respect mean to you? How do you show yourself respect? Acts of self-respect may include creating personal boundaries to help establish your peace and requesting that they be upheld by others; seeking and taking heed of your own advice, rather than relying on an outside opinion; and getting adequate rest so your body and mind remain fresh and energized.

20
JUNE
—
THE SIGNS WILL TELL

When you need help making a decision, ask for a sign to receive confirmation or help. You can determine what the sign is. When you see it, trust and believe that it was meant for you.

21
JUNE
—

I am not afraid of storms for I am learning how to sail my ship.

—*Louisa May Alcott*

22

JUNE

—

MEDITATE IN NATURE

Usually, we close our eyes and go within to meditate. This time, meditate outside. Sit with your eyes open, and notice whatever is around you or what comes your way—a leaf falling from a tree, two squirrels chasing each other, etc. You don't have control over what happens naturally, but you're free to witness the beauty.

23

JUNE

—

WE ARE SUPERHEROES

Your thoughts have power. The power hub is the intentionality behind the thought. The stronger the intention, the more powerful the thought, even against all odds. We all have this power. We are superheroes. What is your theme song?

24
JUNE

SMELL YOUR FLOWERS NOW

Ground yourself in the present moment. Recognize the beauty of your current life. You can celebrate your joys and your wins (no matter how small) each moment they come.

25
JUNE

CURIOUS NATURE

Feel free to break away from your routine or schedule. Be curious and playful. Channel your inner child, and get lost in a different way of thinking. Ask yourself, "How come?"

26
JUNE

—

YOU ARE YOUR PERFECT

If you believe you're already perfect, you don't strive for perfection. You freely live in every moment, knowing that whatever happens is supposed to happen. After all, perfection lies within the eye of the beholder.

27
JUNE

—

AFFIRM THIS THREE TIMES:

I am in charge of my life.
I am living my truths.
I am my ideas.
I am the peace I seek inside.

28
JUNE

———

YOUR MIND IS A GARDEN

Are you planting positive thoughts and beliefs? Are you watering your plants with action? Are you plucking away the pesky weeds?

29
JUNE

———

LIGHT ATTRACTS LIGHT

Go outside. Close your eyes and turn your face to the sun. When you make yourself available, the abundant warmth of the sun's rays will find you. When you show more of the light within you, you will attract more of what's for you.

30
JUNE

EVERY DAY IS A NEW DAY

What is something you loved to do as a child that you don't do anymore? You are grateful for the experience and memories, but you've moved on. You can stop, change, or start over with any decision or belief. Each day, you have the power to do what's best for you.

JULY

*Reestablish the harmony of your mind
and body by remembering the love
that dwells within you, as you.*

1
JULY

LET LOVE FUEL YOU

Listen to your favorite love song. Get lost in the lyrics. Revisit a sweet memory. Love is powerful. When you invite love in, you add a log to your heart's fire.

2
JULY

REST IS ESSENTIAL

When's the last time you took a nap? Rest is an important act of self-love, and it's necessary for rejuvenation. Set a timer, lie down, and drift away into peaceful slumber.

3
JULY

—

CAN YOU DIG IT?

Love gives and receives. Are you blocking that flow? Close your eyes and go within. You may need to do some digging to create a clearer path. Journal about your findings.

4
JULY

—

FREE DAY

You're free to do *whatever* you desire, no conditions. Simply choose to love yourself unconditionally.

5

EAT THE WAY YOU WANT TO THINK

When you eat fresh food, your mind is fresher. Eat something today that is clean: a spinach smoothie, a bowl of fruit, avocado toast, etc.

6

JULY

NUTRITION OF THE MIND

Think about what you're mentally feeding yourself. Is it healthy? Is it junk food that causes you to feel unwell? Do you offer yourself moments to indulge in sweet treats of gratitude? Are you allowing yourself time to properly digest your thoughts before consuming again?

JULY

AFFIRM THIS THREE TIMES:

I am gentle with myself.
I am leading myself in love.
I am love.
I am loved.

JULY

FIND YOUR NATURAL RHYTHM

Go outside. Close your eyes and breathe regularly. Tap into the rhythm of your natural breath. Notice how it exists right along with the song of the birds and the dance of the bees.

9
JULY

—

SEEK AND YOU WILL FIND

Let yourself roam free. You're not lost; you're finding your way home.

10
JULY

—

BE AWARE

Notice your surroundings when you're doing something you love or enjoy.
What do you hear? What do you see, feel, and taste?

11
JULY

MEDITATION TO EMBRACE WISDOM IN LOVE

Close your eyes. Breathe deeply.

Revisit a moment or experience of trauma. Allow yourself to feel the emotions.

Invite in wisdom, and let love enter your heart space on a wave of light.

As the light disperses to illuminate your entire body, ask yourself what you needed in that moment to feel better.

Write your response in your journal.

12
JULY

DATE YOURSELF

Order your favorite meal. Draw a bubble bath for just you. Buy yourself flowers. Go see the latest movie. Take a walk in the park. Whatever it is that you enjoy, spend time alone loving yourself for simply being you.

13
JULY

———

A LOVING REMINDER

Sometimes we can be our own worst critic. We distance ourselves from what we truly want because of fear, failure, or feelings of unworthiness. Place your hand on your heart and remind yourself in love, "No, this is not my truth!"

14
JULY

———

YOU ARE YOUR BEST FRIEND

When you spend more time with yourself in loving thought and conversation, you learn to trust yourself more. Then, when fear or doubt arises, you're more likely to believe in yourself and follow your heart back to love and understanding.

15

JULY

Take a pause
to appreciate how
far you've come.

—*Lalah Delia*

16
JULY

—

ALARMING GRATITUDE

Set an alarm as a reminder to positively affirm yourself. When the alarm sounds, be still in that moment and think of one thing about yourself that you're grateful for.

17
JULY

—

GET IT OUT

Do you ever feel unwillingly attached to someone or some experience from the past, and that feeling leaves a bad taste in your mouth? Spit it out! Seriously. Think of what you want to release, and spit.

18
JULY

MIND STRETCHES

We can carry tensions and limitations in our body that usually correlate with our mind. Begin to stretch your body. Breathe into each stretch, and picture your muscles stretching to block out any negative thought, attitude, or belief that you may have in this moment.

19
JULY

SHARE AND CONNECT

We can become passionate about something that makes us feel more alive and connected with our true spirit. Feel free to share how you feel with others.

20
JULY

—

MEDITATION ON FORGIVENESS

Close your eyes. Breathe deeply.
    Recall a time when you felt that you gave up on yourself.
    Wrap your heart in a blanket of white light.
    Say, "I forgive you."
    Feel the wave of love spread throughout your body.

21
JULY

—

AFFIRM THIS THREE TIMES:

I am making space for myself.
I am open to everything that is for me.
I am free.

22
JULY

A LOVE DONATION

Donate clothing items, jewelry, shoes, or furniture to a friend in need or someone you love. Knowing that your gently loved items will be of use in a home you trust can give you peace of mind when you're revamping your space.

23
JULY

YOUR LOVE IS YOUR TRUTH

Your fears do not define you; they try to control your behavior, but they are not your truth. Let your love be the storyteller of your life.

24
JULY

—

A LOVE LETTER

In your journal, write a list of inner qualities you love about yourself. Describe why you love each of them.

25
JULY

—

WALK BOLDLY

Choose not to be easily distressed or tempted by the words and actions of others. You're free to walk in your power with boldness and confidence.

26
JULY

GIVE YOUR INNER CHILD A GIFT OF LOVE

Give something to yourself today that you remember wanting when you were younger.

27
JULY

To love oneself is the beginning of a life-long romance.

—*Oscar Wilde*

28
JULY

—

YOUR TRIBE CAN AFFECT YOUR VIBE

Take note of how you feel after you connect with someone. Choose wisely those whom you mix with. Your energies may get mixed as well.

29
JULY

—

BEDTIME CLEANSE

Sit still in a comfortable place. Close your eyes.

Imagine yourself surrounded by an energy field that extends six feet from your body in all directions.

Cleanse your energy field using mental visualizations, deep breath exhalations, or intuitive hand movements; or simply be led by your body to create your own unique cleansing practice.

Ground your energy in gratitude by thinking of one thing that occurred today that you are thankful for.

30
JULY

—

PERSONAL SPACE

Bring to mind one room or space in your home that you love. Why do you love it? How does it make you feel? Spend at least an hour in this space, and notice any details that make the space more personal to you.

31
JULY

—

CALL IT LIKE YOU OWN IT

State your goals, desires, or dreams out loud to yourself as if you're living them now. Don't focus on the impossible. Instead, believe the *I'm possible.*

AUGUST

Show yourself love and appreciation for all that you are, and your truest self will be revealed.

1

AUGUST

SHOW LOVE FOR YOUR CONSTANT COMPANION

Place your hand on each part of your body and give thanks. Each part of your body is in connection with your mind, and all work together to support you. Wherever you go, you are always there.

2

AUGUST

YOUR ENERGY IS POWER WITHIN

Be mindful of how you may give away your power to others. Protect your energy. It is certainly helpful to seek outside support and mentorship, but acceptance and validation are ultimately found within.

3

AUGUST

RELAX WITH A MENTAL BREAK

Watch one of your favorite movies. Eat your favorite ice cream. Talk with a good friend. Just relax.

4

AUGUST

LET LOVE IN

Life is so much sweeter when love is present, but sometimes it can be difficult or uncomfortable to receive the gift of love. We might be overwhelmed by thoughts of how to return it before we've even accepted it. Accept the next compliment or show of affection the way flowers accept the rain. Both are acts of love.

5

HOME SWEET HOME

Make a list of how you can show your home unconditional love. It doesn't matter how small, old, disheveled, or outdated you think it is. Consider ways that you can give thanks for its shelter and protection. Now, choose one idea from your list and spread the love.

6

AUGUST

OPEN AND WILLING

Your inner guidance works in all aspects of your life at all times. Listen to the whispers of your inner knowing, and follow the direction of your heart. Trust yourself as a guide to know what is best for you.

7

AUGUST

Write it on your heart that every day is
the best day in the year.

—Ralph Waldo Emerson

8

AUGUST

CIRCLE OF FRIENDS

Are you surrounded by people who accept you for who you are and support
you on your journey toward reaching your goals, or are certain people in your
life projecting their dreams and expectations on you for their own fulfillment? Trust and believe in your self-worth.

9

AUGUST

—

AIR YOUR BREATH

Feel the oxygen circulating through your body as currents of love. Let the oxygen penetrate your mind and your heart, naturally rushing in and flowing to one body part, then the next. Give in to whatever sensation responds to your sweet breeze.

10

AUGUST

—

TEARS OF RELEASE

Grant yourself permission to cry when you need to. Tears are powerful agents of healing and release. After all, it's your life, and you should cry if you want to.

11
AUGUST
—

REMEMBER THE LOVE STORY
WITHIN YOURSELF

This remembrance will allow you to feel secure within yourself and open up to receive love. Love from others is more
fulfilling if you learn to hold yourself in love first.

12
AUGUST

—

BED YOGA

If you are able, try out some yoga in the comfort of your own bed. Some bed-friendly poses include the cobra, cat, and camel poses.

13
AUGUST

—

MEDITATION TO CALL BACK YOUR SOUL INTO WHOLENESS

Close your eyes. Take a few slow, deep breaths.

Envision a string that extends from your heart and connects to something outside of you that is sucking away your energy. This can be a person, a fearful thought, or a traumatic memory.

Using your hands, slowly pull the string back toward your heart, inch by inch, gathering back your energy. Eventually the string will completely unravel and fully return to your heart space, ceasing the connection.

Hold your head high in proud salute as you embrace the fullness of energy that has been restored to you.

14

AUGUST

—

THE EARTH CONNECTS AND GROUNDS US

Go outside and, if you can, place your hands on a tree. Close your eyes and tune inward. Feel the strong, steady energy of the tree rooting you to the support of the Earth.

15
AUGUST

AFFIRM THIS THREE TIMES:

*I am in belief of myself again.
I am focusing on myself with
a loving gaze.
I am returning to my heart.
I am supported.*

16
AUGUST

—

NO MEANS NO

When something or someone in your life requests a *yes* from you, stop and examine your heart. You have the willpower to say *no*. Much growth occurs when you stand firm in who you are.

17
AUGUST

—

PLAY YOUR INSTRUMENT

Listen to a song. As you listen, focus on one instrument in the song. Your instrument—or purpose in being—has a certain vibration that is unique to you in the song of life.

18
AUGUST

—

YOU ARE AN AUTHOR

Imagine you're writing a book about your life. In your journal or notes app, answer these prompts: Who is telling the story? Who are the characters, and why are they here? What is the setting or environment, and how is it unique? Is there a problem or issue? If so, how is it resolved? You can write your story as fiction or nonfiction.

19
AUGUST

—

HOME IS WHERE THE HEART IS

Clean what is considered the heart of the physical home: the kitchen. While you're at it, be mindful of any memories from this space that bring you joy or make you feel loved.

20
AUGUST

—

SPEAK UP FOR YOURSELF IN LOVE

If someone hurts your feelings, be willing to express that with that person. Their intentions may have been harmless, but you still have the authority to speak about how you felt in response.

21
AUGUST

—

The best and most beautiful things in the world cannot be seen or even touched. They must be felt with the heart.

—*Helen Keller*

22

AUGUST

—

BLOCK DISTRACTIONS

Leave your phone behind and go somewhere familiar, a place where you feel safe. The key is to find yourself fully in the moment without distraction. Take in your surroundings. You might be surprised by something that you've never noticed before.

23

AUGUST

—

THANK A FRIEND

Do you have a friend who supports you when you're down or feeling lost? Sometimes, when we're vulnerable, friends help remind us of our worth through acts of kindness and words of love. Check in with a friend with a call, text, or kind thought.

24
AUGUST

—

FACE THE STORM

Sometimes emotions can feel intense, like a heavy storm. Keep in mind that storms bring water to sustain healthy life. Patiently endure the storm.

25
AUGUST

—

EMBRACE YOUR MIND

Close your eyes. Cup your hands together, lean forward, and let your head rest in your hands. Breathe calmly.

26
AUGUST

CONFIDENCE WINS THE GAME

Think back to a moment when you were in control of your creativity. You created based on your original idea, no matter what anyone else thought. What did you create? Where did you find your confidence? Would you do it again?

27
AUGUST

DON'T RUSH THE PROCESS

Be gentle in your unlearning. Although certain beliefs may no longer align with your soul, it took some time for you to adopt them. Likewise, it will take some time for you to let these beliefs go.

28
AUGUST

—

AFFIRM THIS THREE TIMES:

I am patient in loving myself.
I am still growing.
I am remembering and gathering pieces of
myself that make me whole.

29
AUGUST

GUIDE YOURSELF BACK WITH YOUR BREATH

Practice this breathing technique when you feel you're starting to act outside of your true character. Close your eyes. Purse your lips as if you are about to use a straw and draw a deep breath in through your mouth. At the peak of your inhale, hold for three seconds. Release your breath very slowly with a gentle blow. Repeat three times.

30
AUGUST

FORGIVENESS

Hopelessly waiting for others to forgive you is a waste of time and energy. Forgive yourself.

31
AUGUST

PERFECT ATTENDANCE

Show up for yourself each day with love and compassion. You are a student in the school of life. Each day, you learn more about yourself and how you connect with the world. You can do this. You are doing this.

SEPTEMBER

*Verbalize your truths with confidence
and freedom of expression.
You are the spokesperson for your
authentic brand.*

1

SEPTEMBER

—

HUM A TUNE

Hum to yourself while you're working or doing chores. Relaxing to a controlled rhythm helps your energy flow, bypassing that traffic jam in your mind.

2

SEPTEMBER

—

YOUR NAME IS MEANINGFUL

Create an acronym using the letters in your first name. Write it down and put it in a visible place in your bedroom. This will remind you that your name alone is a strong instrument—one that holds the vastness of who you are.

3

SEPTEMBER

—

SPA BATH

Add 10 drops of your favorite essential oil to your bath water, and relax. Aromatherapy can help calm and soothe our energy, especially after a long day of thought and action.

4

SEPTEMBER

—

SCREAM IT OUT

When you're struggling with or feeling overwhelmed by a tough moment in the day, try releasing your pent-up energy by screaming into a pillow or laughing a big belly laugh—whatever feels right for you. To boost confidence and eliminate regret, give yourself the freedom to express your frustrations in a healthy way.

5
SEPTEMBER

FREE-WRITE

Sit for 5 to 10 minutes and journal about whatever freely comes to mind. You don't need intentions or question prompts—just write on.

6
SEPTEMBER

CLAIM YOUR EXISTENCE

Think of one thing you would do or say if you had no fear of denial, rejection, ridicule, or judgment. Your existence is greater than any limiting thought. Exist boldly. Exist truly. Exist still.

7

SEPTEMBER

—

AFFIRM THIS THREE TIMES:

*I am an important voice in this world.
I am not afraid to speak my mind.
I am aware of my thoughts and speak them
with truth.*

8

SEPTEMBER

—

JUST SING

Sing in the shower or car. Use your voice. Hear it.

9

LISTEN AND LEARN

Listen to a podcast, music album, or audible reading that speaks to you and applies to your interests. Listening to creative art shared by others can inspire you to embrace and embody your own unique, creative insight.

10

SEPTEMBER

WHAT'S YOUR MOTTO?

Create a quote or slogan about yourself. Feel free to use one of your personal learning experiences as inspiration.

11
SEPTEMBER

—

A MOMENT OF SILENCE

Choose two hours of the day to spend time in silence—no talking, no music, no TV, no phone. Silence dismisses the noise that can distract you and take your attention away from the small voice of truth inside you.

12
SEPTEMBER

—

SAY IT LOUD

When you feel overwhelmed or discouraged, say out loud to yourself, "Yes, I can. Yes, I am!"

13

SEPTEMBER

—

CURSE *SOMETHING* OUT INSTEAD OF *SOMEONE* OUT

When someone evokes an unpleasant emotion from you, this serves as a mirror to reflect the emotion rooted in you from one of your personal experiences. Curse out those things that are trying to rob you, keep you small, or sabotage your willingness to receive your abundance.

14

SEPTEMBER

—

SHARE YOUR PERSPECTIVE

Before bedtime, share what happened over the course of your entire day. You can share your experiences with someone, or you can write about these experiences in your journal.

15
SEPTEMBER
—

The ability to simplify means
to eliminate the unnecessary so
that the necessary may speak.

—Hans Hofmann

16
SEPTEMBER
—

COMMUNICATE WHAT TYPE OF ENERGY
YOU WANT IN YOUR HOME

Speak it over a particular room or space, and make an intention to maintain
that vibe. For instance, you may declare that your bedroom is a private space
where love, trust, and intimacy thrive. You maintain that home vibration by
only inviting in those people or experiences that are specifically aligned with
that energy.

SEPTEMBER

MEDITATION FOR RECLAIMING YOUR FREEDOM

Close your eyes.

Take three deep breaths.

Think of a moment from your childhood when you were forced to keep your feelings and beliefs to yourself.

On your next exhale, let out a loud, audible sigh to release the restraint on your freedom of expression.

Repeat as many times as you like—and if you need to roar it out like a lion, go for it!

18
SEPTEMBER

ONE FINE DAY

In your journal, describe what a perfect day would look like to you, from the time you wake, until the moment you fall asleep.

19
SEPTEMBER

GIVE WHAT YOU WISH TO RECEIVE

When you're having a conversation with someone, choose to simply listen. Listen with genuine interest so you feel or see what the person is describing. Your listening presence fosters an appreciation for who the person is, instead of what that person provides for you.

20
SEPTEMBER

—

LISTEN INTENTLY

Place yourself in a comfortable position. Choose a short singing bowl video on YouTube. These ancient bowls are made of different metals and produce sound through vibrations when they are struck or scraped. Singing bowls are often used for meditation because they help focus the mind and promote deep relaxation. Sit still, close your eyes, and simply listen.

21
SEPTEMBER

—

AFFIRM THIS THREE TIMES:

I am in confident expression of myself.
I am a voice that is waiting to be heard.
I am creative by just being me.

22
SEPTEMBER

—

HOME EXPRESSION

Embrace what may be unique or different about your physical home as you make it your own expression of art. Maybe it's a TV in the kitchen, a landline phone connection, or a mirror above the bed. You're free to claim your space in this world with authenticity.

23
SEPTEMBER

—

EMBODY YOUR TRUTH

If you are able, alternate between your favorite yoga poses or stretches. As you enter into each pose, recite the So Hum mantra which means, "I am that". Say: *Soo – Humm.* This mantra helps ground you and increases focus on your journey.

24

—

BRIDGE THE GAP

When you're living mindfully, a bridge connects the intuitive needs and wants of your heart to the active language of the mind. What does your bridge look like or mean to you? Is it intact, crumbling, or nonexistent?

25

SEPTEMBER

—

JOURNAL DETECTIVE

Whenever you become aware of how you're feeling or thinking about something today, take a brief moment to jot it down. If it's easier, write a bulleted list instead of full sentences. Think of your feelings as mental clues.

26
SEPTEMBER

—

ASK FOR HELP

Allow yourself to receive help. You are worth it, and you are loved.

27
SEPTEMBER

—

Speak with integrity.
Use the power of your
word in the direction
of truth and love.

—Don Miguel Ruiz

28
SEPTEMBER

WRITE AND RELEASE

Are you anxious about sharing your inner thoughts and feelings with others?
Write a letter or note to express yourself in a more safe and comfortable way.
Just writing down your thoughts can be such a powerful release for your
mind, even if you never send the letter.

29
SEPTEMBER

CLOUD NINE

Venture outside and look up at the sky. Notice how it remains still and steady
as the clouds float along, changing shape. Think of those clouds as your
thoughts or values. Allow those that no longer align with who you are to float
away from your sky as you welcome new clouds of creativity and inspiration.

30
SEPTEMBER

DOUBLE YOUR PLEASURE

Write down two things you're thankful for. Read each one
aloud. After you read each one, close your eyes and allow
yourself a moment to feel why you are thankful.

OCTOBER

You have the ability to speak your mind and communicate your creative expression. Your unique voice is the mouthpiece for your purpose.

1
OCTOBER

—

JET LAG

Do you find yourself delaying the start or completion of a task, despite being aware of the possible negative consequences of this hesitation? Make a list of habits that you turn to when you procrastinate. When such a moment arises again, you're more likely to notice the habit and rise above it.

2
OCTOBER

—

WIND DOWN OVERACTIVE ENERGY

Close your eyes. Slowly roll your neck to the left 10 times. Then, roll your neck 10 times to the right. Focus on the gentle movement of your body, and give your mind a rest.

3

OCTOBER

AN UNFORGETTABLE MEMORY

Think of one thing that you like or appreciate and will never forget. Maybe it's a song, a commercial jingle, dialogue in a movie, or a dance move. Many things change as years go by, but some memories stay put. Over time, you may recognize yourself—or you may not. But oh how sweet it is when you realize that you can never forget how to be who you are.

4

OCTOBER

MINDFUL BREATHING

With each inhale, think about air coming in. With each exhale, think about air going out. Thoughts or distractions may come. When they do, observe and thank them. Let them pass. Embrace the calm and confidence of your life-sustaining breath.

5
OCTOBER

YOUR VOICE IS A NOTE

Do you ever listen to the sound of your voice? How does it make you feel? Record your voice as you sing, read, rap, or whisper. The sound of your voice is authentically yours and is a beautiful note to life's song.

6
OCTOBER

LISTENING EARS

Call a friend today and make a point to listen more than you talk. Listening to others helps you develop control over your thoughts and how you share them. Paying thoughtful attention to someone else allows you to develop more patience when your mind is full of thoughts.

7
OCTOBER

—

AFFIRM THIS THREE TIMES:

I am attractive for what is right for me.
I am able to receive my desires.

8
OCTOBER

—

BE HONEST WITH YOURSELF

Have you ever held on to something because you think, "One day I might need it"? Then, the clutter around your home begins to rebuild. Will you truly need that one thing again? Consider the deeper reasoning behind why you feel you can't let it go.

9
OCTOBER

—

1, 2, 3: SCREAM!

Scream at the top of your lungs. It doesn't have to be scary or sad. Screaming breaks up your thought pattern and can help you assert confidence and stand up for yourself (even when you are your own challenger).

10
OCTOBER

—

IT'S IN YOUR HANDS

If you're able, use your hands to create something. Prepare a meal. Doodle. Paint your nails. Play the piano. Your hands (like your mind) have their own language and are messengers of your soul.

11

—

GIVE BIRTH TO YOUR IDEAS

Do you have creative ideas but struggle to bring them to life? Believe that you can attain your creative desires. Trust in your belief with aligned action. This is the blueprint that gives form to your creations.

12

—

SHARING IS CARING

Give someone a *genuine* compliment today. It will feel good to connect with others, especially when your honest opinion is recognized and received.

13

OCTOBER

DON'T FORGET TO REST

Take a nap with binaural beats playing in your headphones.

14

OCTOBER

HYPE IT UP

Your words matter—those that you speak to yourself and others. Think of yourself as a best friend (named Confidence) who reminds you of how awesome you are and affirms what has already been shared in your heart.

15

OCTOBER

—

Listen to silence. It has much to say.

—*Rumi*

16

OCTOBER

—

IT'S A *YES* FOR ME

People-pleasing can lead to an unhealthy *yes* when you do things merely to make other people happy. You may end up giving your power and influence away to others. *Yes* is not a doormat—it's an affirmation. Is your *yes* affirming who you are and what you believe?

17

OCTOBER

—

DEEP BELLY BREATHS

Place one hand on your belly. Take a deep breath, and feel your belly rise with air. When you've taken your full breath, release it slowly and feel your belly deflate. Embrace the calmness throughout your body, and set an intention to refresh your mind.

18
OCTOBER

PARTS OF A WHOLE

Think of one adjective to describe each of these parts of your being: mind, body, heart, and soul. Create "I am" affirmations using each adjective.

19
OCTOBER

THE FREEDOM OF SPEECH

When you come across a thought that grabs your full attention, verbalize it. Talk it out. Talk through it with yourself. You may feel more integrated with your mind when you can speak what you think without judgment or restraint.

20
OCTOBER

—

CONFIDE IN YOURSELF

Confidence can affect how we feel about ourselves and how much we believe in our efforts. What makes you feel confident? Is it doing something you like? Arriving prepared? Studying to gain knowledge? Creating something new? Helping others find their way?

21
OCTOBER

—

AFFIRM THIS THREE TIMES:

I am safe to express my thoughts and opinions.
I am not intimidated by the world beyond me.
I am unique and valuable.

22
OCTOBER

—

WHAT'S GOOD FOR YOU WILL STICK AROUND

Make sticky-note reminders of your favorite quotes or affirmations that are important to you and what you believe. Place them around your home where you're sure to notice them.

23
OCTOBER

—

FREE-FLOW MEDITATION

Close your eyes.

Take a few deep breaths.

Don't try to fight off any thoughts or visions—let whatever comes across your mind enter and exit without judgment or force.

Your thoughts are welcome to flow freely and naturally in this sacred space of your mind. Often, restlessness in our minds is reduced when we give each thought time to identify itself completely.

24
OCTOBER

—

GET MAD ABOUT IT

Anger is an intense emotion that can be alchemized into passion. Add more fuel to the fire. Add more fuel to your desires.

25
OCTOBER

—

DEEP CLEANING

Choose one small area within your home and give it a thorough cleaning. Sometimes we have to show attention to those minor details that tend to get overlooked on a daily basis. Baseboards, door handles, window blinds, and ceiling fans are important pieces of the home that need TLC.

26
OCTOBER

A WORK OF ART

Take a look in the mirror. Speak positively about yourself. Pay attention to your choice of words. You can be as creative or poetic as you desire. Here's an example: "My eyes are like matching buttons sewn along the string of my heart." Now, you try!

27
OCTOBER

Believe you can, and you're halfway there.

—*Theodore Roosevelt*

28
OCTOBER

MEDITATION ON GROUNDING YOUR ENERGY

Recall places to which you have traveled all over the country or world. Allow roots from the base of your spine to venture out from where you sit and connect with each place you have been.

Feel the rejuvenating energy seep up through your roots, flowing up the river of your spine until it bursts forth, covering you with a rain shower of peace and wholeness.

29
OCTOBER

YES, I CAN

Your words are powerful manifesting agents. When you say "I can't," you align yourself with that negative energy. Speak positive "I can" statements about your life, and believe that they are true. You have the power to create your future.

30
OCTOBER

—

RISE FROM YOUR ASHES

Cast out what does not speak to you, what doesn't align with your truths, and what doesn't serve your best interests. Doing so is not a weakness; it's a freedom. Rise up for yourself.

31

OCTOBER

TRICK OR TREAT

Don't be afraid to express your truth to the world. What you think may be tricky for others to understand might be just the treat they've been waiting for.

NOVEMBER

Your intuition is a helpful guide along your journey. Embrace the insight that comes from your experiences, and life will feel more at ease.

1

NOVEMBER

—

PACE YOURSELF

It's okay to take time to see where you want to be. This is an opportunity for you to love on yourself even more—and, like time, it never has to end.

2

NOVEMBER

—

THE HIGH LIFE

Visualize your highest self, and show up today in that essence. Move talk, eat, think, dream, and be in that awareness of self.

3
NOVEMBER

WHAT WILL BE, WILL BE

Do you ever obsess over something you want to have happen in your life? Cease the chase. Create more space for it to arrive in your life. Do this by seeing it and claiming it as yours. Then, free it from your mind. Trust that it will work out as it should and resist the urge to focus on or visualize a particular outcome.

4
NOVEMBER

WONDER IN A HIGHER PERSPECTIVE

Spend some time outside and turn your gaze upward.

5
NOVEMBER

KNOW WHEN TO SAY *NO*

When you get to know yourself better, you realize what is true of your genuine self—and what is not. Own who you are, and say *no* to anything that lies outside your true nature.

6
NOVEMBER

THE SWEET LIFE

Eat a piece of dark chocolate. It helps enhance mental clarity and boost concentration.

NOVEMBER

AFFIRM THIS THREE TIMES:

I am on my true path.
I am following the lead of my inner teacher.
I am the source of my truth.

8

NOVEMBER

A TRUE VISION OF BEAUTY

Society's idea of beauty usually involves a small waist. There is less emphasis on the *waste* of the mind. I invite you to find true beauty in the shape of your mind.

9
NOVEMBER

—

MEDITATION FOR MANIFESTING YOUR DESIRES

Close your eyes.

Take three deep breaths.

Visualize something or an experience you want in your life.

Become aware of how you feel. Embody that feeling.

When you're ready, express gratitude for where you are now and what's to come.

10
NOVEMBER

—

YOUR COMPASS IS WITHIN

The journey to discover what is meant for you in life doesn't have to be uncomfortable. There is wisdom in ease. You may not be able to fully see the end destination, but the path feels right. Your *in-sight* (how you feel within) is a helpful compass on your journey.

11
NOVEMBER

—

GO TO BED EARLIER

Aim to get seven to eight hours of uninterrupted sleep so you'll wake up feeling rejuvenated and clearheaded.

12
NOVEMBER

—

WHAT IF?

There's always some truth in your imagination. Get as wild as you want, and create a world of your own from your imagination. What color is the sky? What does the air smell like? How do you communicate?

13
NOVEMBER

—

CHILL AND HEAL

Position yourself into a favorite stretch or yoga pose that is very comfortable to you. The child pose is a good option. Close your eyes and breathe normally. Stay in this position for at least 5 minutes or longer, without moving. Allow thoughts or emotions to come and go, but remain still and steady in your body.

14
NOVEMBER

—

GREET THE PURPOSE OF TODAY

Release the need to make things happen in a certain way at a certain time. Ground yourself in your present reality and how you feel in this moment. How you live today is how you relate to tomorrow.

15
NOVEMBER

—

Edit your life frequently
and ruthlessly. It's your
masterpiece after all.

—Nathan W. Morris

16
NOVEMBER

OUT OF SIGHT, OUT OF MIND

If you can't see yourself living the life you desire, how can you believe that you can have it? It's a lot like seeing a neat idea and feeling inspired to create something in your home. Get started! Organize your closet. Create a wall collage of framed pictures. Repurpose an old furniture piece.

17
NOVEMBER

YOUR BODYGUARD

You are in communication with yourself every day—such as when your body tells you that you're hungry or that you need to use the restroom. Or maybe you feel a nudge to take a different route home or to check on a family member. Embrace your intuition as a helpful guide.

18
NOVEMBER

MEDITATION TO FOSTER ACCEPTANCE OF GUT FEELINGS

Close your eyes. Take three deep breaths.

Place your left hand on your heart and your right hand on your belly.

As your belly (gut) rises on your inhale, envision it being full of your true feelings.

When you exhale, visualize the insight traveling to your heart and then being released out into the universe.

19
NOVEMBER

EAT CLEAN FOOD

Processed food contains fillers that are not helpful to your body. Less is more. Consider food like fresh fruit, hummus and veggies, whole grains, avocados, and nuts. A clearer body helps facilitate a clearer mind.

20
NOVEMBER

—

THE PAST IS IN THE PAST

You don't have to be consumed by what used to be—you can choose to see the now. See your growth, courage, and strength. This gives you the power to see the true lesson in what used to be.

21
NOVEMBER

—

AFFIRM THIS THREE TIMES:

I am a well of wisdom.
I am a truth seeker.
I am open to inspiration.
I am here for a reason.

22
NOVEMBER

—

SOMETHING NEW

Try a new activity that you wouldn't have considered doing before. This will help keep you curious to learn more about yourself.

23
NOVEMBER

—

CHOOSE YOURSELF

Our minds can be so indecisive when we try to make simple decisions—and even more so when we're deciding how to live in our purpose. Take one decision at a time. You have lots of opportunities to practice your free will, from choosing what to wear in the morning to deciding what to eat for dinner. It's not about right or wrong—it's about what you learn about yourself.

24
NOVEMBER

—

MEDITATE WITH YOUR FAVORITE COLOR

Close your eyes.

Make a soft fist with each hand, curling your index fingers over your thumbs.

Take three deep breaths. Relax and envision one of your favorite colors. It can be the color itself, a field of flowers in that color, or maybe a sunset. You are surrounded by the colorful energy of love.

25
NOVEMBER

—

KEEP CALM AND VISION-BOARD

Create a Pinterest or mood board to reimagine how to decorate a new, clean space in your home. When you can visualize it beforehand, it's easier to bring to life a room that carries the energy of your heart's desires.

26

DREAM CATCHER

Set an intention before bed to remember your dreams. Whenever you wake—in the morning or in the middle of the night—record any details you remember. Try to recall the scene, the characters, the colors, the smells, and how you felt. Your dreams can help you understand more about your present life.

27

NOVEMBER

———

It's not what you look at that matters. It's what you see.

—Henry David Thoreau

28

NOVEMBER

———

YOU ARE LIMITLESS

Silence the inner voice that makes you feel less than the magical being you are. Often, it's the voice of your ego, which is trying to "protect" you and keep you within the safety of your comfort zone. Break free of any limiting beliefs, and dream higher.

29

NOVEMBER

—

A BIRD'S-EYE VIEW

When you feel overwhelmed or confused, slow down. Create distance between yourself and your current situation by rising above it. Allow yourself to see the larger perspective of it all.

30

NOVEMBER

—

A HEAD IN THE CLOUDS

We can get lost in our daydreams and use them to escape from reality. Ground yourself in your present energy here on Earth. Connect your thoughts back to the reality of your life. This is the anchor that will help balance out your moments of flight.

DECEMBER

You've made it this far on your journey! This is just the beginning. You are the home. Every day is up to you. Live on. Live mindfully.

1

DECENTER

—

YOU ARE A WHOLE VIBE

What does your vibe sound like? What does it feel like, taste like, and smell like?

2

DECEMBER

—

DRINK MORE WATER

Quench your thirst.

3
DECEMBER

YOU ARE THE JUDGE

Whenever you have *any* thought, you hold the power to question it. You can welcome each incoming statement to the court of your heart and require evidence to prove its truth.

4
DECEMBER

EYES-WIDE-OPEN MEDITATION

Keep your eyes open. Be present in the moment. Softly stare at whatever you choose: a flower, a candle, a picture of your family, etc. Witness the miracles that are already embedded in your life in the simplest ways.

5

DECEMBER

———

SOUL FAMILY

Spend time (via phone call, video call, or physical meetup) with those people in your life who are like soul family. The sharing of a deep connection and divine sustenance comes from each of you communicating simply who you are.

6

DECEMBER

———

HAVE YOU NOTICED ANYTHING DIFFERENT LATELY?

Signs (numbers, animals, songs) appear to communicate different things to you, like, "Look at you, living an abundant life, one mindful moment at a time!"

7
DECEMBER

—

AFFIRM THIS THREE TIMES:

I am guided by something greater than myself.
I am part of the big picture.
I am one with my true nature.

8
DECEMBER

—

MIND FULL

Choose a three-hour period during the day to refrain from eating anything.
Be nourished by your thoughts instead of by food.

9
DECEMBER

—

WHEN YOU HELP OTHERS, YOU HELP YOURSELF

Volunteer to help organize or clean a space in the home of a friend or family member. Your efforts will be appreciated and will likely help inspire you to do the same for yourself.

10
DECEMBER

—

SILENT TREATMENT

Sit in a comfortable spot—no phone, no movement, no meditation. Just be still and silent with yourself for 10 minutes.

11
DECEMBER

—

WE ALL ARE DIFFERENT, AND THAT MAKES US THE SAME

A crucial part of appreciating your own unique beliefs is recognizing how your beliefs may differ from the beliefs of others. You don't have to adopt or agree with them—just accept that their beliefs may be different from yours. We each take up space in the tapestry of this world.

12
DECEMBER

—

YOGA IS LIFE

Get your yoga on. Try the lotus pose, seated forward bend, or tree pose.

13
DECEMBER

—

YOU KNOW YOURSELF BEST

Limiting thoughts or beliefs will occur—but as you become stronger, those thoughts and beliefs become weaker. Now, when you think these kinds of negative thoughts, you can ask yourself how to work through them. Meditate? Go outside? Cry? Orgasm?

14
DECEMBER

—

TAP INTO EMOTIONAL FREEDOM

Using your hands and fingertips, tap on the areas of your body that call to you. Say out loud or think to yourself, "I am love, and I receive love." This technique is a helpful release that can help move energy blocks when you come up against limiting beliefs or emotions.

15
DECEMBER
—

Not all those who
wander are lost.

—*J.R.R. Tolkien*

16
DECEMBER

—

A LOVE CONNECTION

Your unconditional love for yourself naturally connects with your love for others. Consider how you have more understanding and compassion for someone who is on the journey home to themselves, but who might be struggling in the moment. You've been there before—maybe a different circumstance, but you can recognize that the emotion is the same.

17
DECEMBER

—

READ OUTSIDE

Grab an enjoyable book and venture outside. If you can, find a good spot with ample sunlight.

18

DECEMBER

—

BE AWARE OF YOUR ATMOSPHERE

When you feel yourself retreating to a thought pattern or habit that no longer serves you, immediately check your surroundings for visuals that might be affecting you. Are you scrolling on a particular Instagram page? Are you seeing disturbing news on TV? When you're able to shine a light on the shadow, it's easier to clear it from your mind.

19

DECEMBER

—

BACKSEAT DRIVER

By now, you've had many days of practice and mindful awareness, and it may have become easier to trust yourself in your decisions. You can naturally let go of the wheel and relax in the back seat of your mind.

20

DECEMBER

—

SACRED SPACE

Dedicate an area in your home as your sacred space. This is where you feel most comfortable practicing your mindfulness rituals, like meditation, journaling, and silent contemplation. Decorate or enhance this space in a way that makes you feel calm, peaceful, and in connection with your truest expression of self.

21

DECEMBER

—

AFFIRM THIS THREE TIMES:

I am insightful.
I am letting my light shine.
I am ready to live my life.
I am at peace.

22

—

MINDFUL GROWTH

What behaviors or old patterns are you holding on to that no longer serve you in your growth? With each arriving breath, call in the energy of growth and self-realization to clear out those outdated constructs. Make space for new designs to take form.

23

DECEMBER

—

WITNESS YOUR MIND

Set an intention or repeat a favorite affirmation before you journal. Ground your energy using slow and deep breathing. You can even play light music to set the energy of the space. Write whatever comes into your thoughts.

24
DECEMBER

—

YOUR ENERGY IS SHARED TO RELATE, NOT DISSIPATE

You can listen to someone without taking on their cares. When you choose to listen, you can simply be a genuine presence instead of trying to solve another person's problem.

25
DECEMBER

—

FORGIVENESS IS A GIFT

Think back to an individual or circumstance that you feel held you back or limited your free expression in some way. Now, say out loud, "I forgive you."

26
DECEMBER

—

GIVE YOURSELF A HAND

If you can, give yourself a face massage using your hands. This has physical benefits, of course, but it also calms the mind by helping relieve tension, stress, and anxiety. Your hands can turn back time in more ways than one.

27
DECEMBER

—

LOVE IS YOU

The reservoir lives in you. When you feel a healthy desire to give love or to receive it, do so freely. Simply being you replenishes your supply.

28

DECEMBER

—

TREAT YOURSELF

Do something that you find fun or exciting. Swipe right on Tinder. Watch the latest episode of a good Netflix series. Get ice cream after dinner. Little treats like these help sustain your energy and reconnect you with the pleasure of life.

29

DECEMBER

—

MEET AND GREET

How would it be for your past you to meet you now? What would that interaction look like?

30
DECEMBER

—

Wisdom begins
at the end.

—*Daniel Webster*

31

DECEMBER

—

YOUR HOME IS ALWAYS WITH YOU

Give thanks for how far you've come. You can go anywhere
in the world and feel at home just by being you. Now, imagine
how far you can go.

RESOURCES

WEBSITES

BecomingMinimalist.com
Helpful articles about minimalist living to guide beginners.

TheMinimalists.com
Books, podcasts, Netflix series, and free e-books for the minimalist.

SovereignSoulMedicine.com and FaeryEssence.com
Two online ritual shops full of tools to help support you along the daily journey of mindfulness.

JeralynGlass.com
A library of beautiful sound meditations using crystal bowls.

BOOKS

Vibrate Higher Daily: Live Your Power, **by Lalah Delia**
Warm guidance and affirmations to cultivate a lifestyle by remembering who you are and rising into that potential each day; inspiration for you to embrace your inner creativity.

The Emotion Code: How to Release Your Trapped Emotions for Abundant Health, Love, and Happiness, **by Dr. Bradley Nelson**
Techniques to help release emotions and beliefs that no longer serve you.

APPS

Calm
Soothing meditations and music that help calm your energy.

OfferUp
A mobile marketplace to let go of anything you no longer want or need.

Skillshare
Free classes that empower you to remain curious and learn new things that bring you joy.

INSTAGRAM

@maryamhasnaa
Inspirational quotes

@alex_elle
Inspirational affirmations

@pushingbeauty
Self-love reminders

@phyllicia.bonanno
Inspiration for mindful movement in yoga

@josiahbell
DJ vibes that will have you dancing and moving your energy.

MUSIC

Mantras in Love, **by Beautiful Chorus**
Music for meditation and grounding your energy to come back home.

Stay Free, **by Londrelle**
Music mantras for conscious-minded living.

REFERENCES

"101 Chakra Quotes." *LexiYoga*. LexiYoga.com/chakra-quotes.

Addis, Kristin. "Crown Chakra: Everything You Need to Know." *Be My Travel Muse*. February 14, 2021. BeMyTravelMuse.com/crown-chakra.

Barrett, Suzi. *The Chakras Activity Book & Journal*. Knock Knock, 2019.

Beckler, Melanie. "23 Ways to Heal Your Root Chakra." *Ask Angels*. Ask-Angels.com/spiritual-guidance/23-ways-heal-root-chakra.

Cooper, Sarah. "7 Ways to Heal the Heart Chakra." *Gathering of Minds*. ourgom.com/7-ways-to-heal-the-heart-chakra.

Dadabhay, Yasmin. "10 Signs Your Throat Chakra Is Opening." *Subconscious Servant*. SubconsciousServant.com/throat-chakra-opening-signs.

Delia, Lalah. *Vibrate Higher Daily: Live Your Power*. HarperOne, 2019.

Dienstman, Allison Michelle. "Chakra Healing: How to Open Your Throat Chakra." *Goodnet*. August 15, 2019. GoodNet.org/articles /chakra-healing-how-to-open-your-throat.

Dimas, Jessica. "Sacred Self-Care for Sacral Chakra Healing." *Jessica Dimas*. August 13, 2019. JessicaDimas.com/sacred-self-care-for-healing-your -sacral-chakra.

Hathaway, Miriam. *Simply Grateful*. Compendium, 2018.

Hurst, Katherine. "Chakra Healing for Beginners: How to Open Your Third Eye." *The Law of Attraction*. TheLawOfAttraction.com/third-eye -chakra-healing.

Hurst, Katherine. "Sacral Chakra Healing for Beginners: How to Open Your Sacral Chakra." *The Law of Attraction*. TheLawOfAttraction.com /sacral-chakra-healing.

Jai, Tiffany. "Minimalism Quotes That Inspire You to Simplify." *Be Bright and Shine*. BeBrightAndShine.com/minimalism-quotes.

Koniver, Laura. "8 Ways to (Almost) Instant Throat Chakra Healing." *Intuition Physician*. October 1, 2012. Intuition-Physician.com/8-ways-to-almost -instant-throat-chakra-healing.

Luna, Aletheia. "The Ultimate Guide to Root Chakra Healing for Complete Beginners." *Lonerwolf*. June 12, 2021. LonerWolf.com /root-chakra-healing.

Luna, Aletheia. "The Ultimate Guide to Sacral Chakra Healing for Complete Beginners." *Lonerwolf*. June 12, 2021. LonerWolf.com/sacral-chakra -healing.

Luna, Aletheia. "The Ultimate Guide to Solar Plexus Chakra Healing for Complete Beginners." *Lonerwolf*. December 26, 2020. LonerWolf.com /solar-plexus-chakra-healing.

Luna, Aletheia. "The Ultimate Guide to Throat Chakra Healing for Complete Beginners." *Lonerwolf*. June 12, 2021. LonerWolf.com/throat-chakra -healing.

Maree, Jordane, et al [@girlandhermoon]. "New Moon in Aries." *Instagram*. April 11, 2021. Instagram.com/p/CNhlaBmHKYI/?utm_medium=copy_link.

"Minimalism Quotes." *Good Reads*. Goodreads.com/quotes/tag/minimalism.

Olsgard, Meghan. "Third Eye Chakra Blockages – 6 Ways to Heal the Sixth Chakra." *Infinite Soul Blueprint* InfiniteSoulBlueprint.com/third -eye-chakra-blockages-6-ways-to-heal-the-sixth-chakra.

Russell, Melissa. "Minimalism and Mindfulness: 4 Ways They Make an Excellent Pair." *Simple Lionheart Life*. June 25, 2017. SimpleLionheartLife .com/minimalism-and-mindfulness.

Sharpe, Rachel. "150+ Mindfulness Quotes to Help You Live More Mindfully." *Declutter The Mind*. February 12, 2021. DeclutterTheMind.com/blog /mindfulness-quotes.

Singh, Jagjot. "7 Signs of Throat (Vishuddha) Chakra Blockage." *Mindfulness Quest*. MindfulnessQuest.com/throat-chakra-blockage.

Singh, Jagjot. "Healing the Solar Plexus (Manipura) Chakra Blockage." *Mindfulness Quest*. MindfulnessQuest.com/healing-solar-plexus-chakra -blockage.

Singh, Jagjot. "Unblocking The Root Chakra ~ Beginner's Guide to Survival, Safety & Vitality." *Mindfulness Quest*. MindfulnessQuest.com/root -chakra-healing.

Tiwari, Harsh. "Top 50 Minimalism Quotes on Simplicity in Life." *Brilliant Read*. June 6, 2020. BrilliantRead.com/minimalism-quotes-on-simplicity -in-life.

White, Jennifer. "6 Simple Ways to Balance Your Root Chakra." *Mind Body Green*. November 11, 2020. MindBodyGreen.com/0-4514/6-Simple-Ways -to-Balance-Your-Root-Chakra.html.

INDEX

ACKNOWLEDGMENTS

To my spiritual team that guides and supports me every day, I am grateful for the unconditional love and support. Thank you for helping me come home to myself each time.

To my dear husband, thank you for believing in me before I even believed in myself. You helped me realize that *I can*, because *I am*!

To my son, Dash, who is curious by nature and creative by design. No one and nothing can stop you from pursuing your passions.

To my daughter, Harlow, my little woman—you teach me every day how to live life with wonder and awe. You, bright star, are my muse.

To my family and friends, thank you for the words of love, hope, kindness, and truth. You helped speak life into my dreams.

To myself, I see you. And I love you forever.

ABOUT THE AUTHOR

 **Tia Patterson** is a wife, a mother of two, and a woman who lives life authentically in her purpose. She is an attorney, YouTube vlogger, blogger, and writer. She strives to embody her true identity and, as she grows and evolves over time, she identifies a little bit more of herself. Nothing is off limits. All things are possible. Just by being yourself. *Be you.* It's her love message to herself and anyone else who chooses to believe.

CPSIA information can be obtained
at www.ICGtesting.com
Printed in the USA
BVHW061654041221
622706BV00003B/3